Fl

by Kris Bonnell

Flamingos are pink birds.
They live by the water.

Flamingos are tall.
They have long, thin legs.

Flamingos can stand in deep water.

Flamingos can swim very well.
They have webbed feet.

Flamingos can fly.

Flamingos eat lots of shrimp.
Shrimp are pink.
Eating shrimp makes
flamingos pink, too.

Baby flamingos are called chicks.
They are born gray.
Chicks have to eat lots
of shrimp to become pink.

chick
flamingo
shrimp
webbed feet